RICHARD PLATT is a renowned non-fiction writer whose previous titles
include *Pirate Diary* (Walker) illustrated by Chris Riddell, which won
the 2002 Kate Greenaway Medal. Its predecessor, *Castle Diary,*
was shortlisted for the same prize as well as for the Kurt Maschler Award
and the *History Today* prize. His collaboration with Stephen Biesty led to
half a dozen books in the Cross-Sections series for Dorling Kindersley:
the first, *Incredible Cross Sections,* was shortlisted for the Smarties Prize,
and the last, *Incredible Body,* for the Rhône Poulenc Prize.
He has written twenty other other titles for DK
including *Cinema, Pirate* and *Spy* in the Eyewitness Guides series,
and *Everest* and *Aztec* in the Eyewitness Discovery series.


RUPERT VAN WYK is a widely-travelled illustrator whose books include
*A Song for Planet Earth,* written by Meredith Hooper (OUP, 1999),
*Sharks* (OUP, 2000) and *The Kickstart Students' Book* (OUP, 2001).
Working on *The Vanishing Rainforest* has inspired him to visit
South America and see the rainforest for himself.

# For Hamish, Freya and Elissa – R.P.

First published in Great Britain in 2003 by
Frances Lincoln Children's Books, 4 Torriano Mews,
Torriano Avenue, London NW5 2RZ
www.franceslincoln.com

First paperback edition 2004

British Library Cataloguing in Publication Data available on request

ISBN 978-0-7112-2170-3 (UK)
ISBN 978-1-84507-321-3 (USA)

Set in Stone Sans Semibold

Printed in Singapore

3 5 7 9 8 6 4

# The Vanishing Rainforest

RICHARD PLATT

Illustrated by RUPERT VAN WYK

F

FRANCES LINCOLN
CHILDREN'S BOOKS

Remaema walked lazily through the rainforest towards the river, sucking her favourite wild berries. At the water's edge she washed her sticky hands. The muddy water hurried past her to join the world's largest river – the Amazon.

Remaema heard a noise. It sounded like an insect close to her ear, but it came from the distant river bank. When the buzzing stopped, the tree-tops moved, and one of the tallest trees fell.

She hurried home and told her mother what she had seen.

"Child, it is the *nabë*. You heard the machine they use to cut trees."

Remaema nodded. The nabë were white people – strangers. They had come to take away her forest.

As the sun set, Remaema's uncle Moawa returned to the *yano* – the round house which all the families shared. He proudly carried a new *machete*, and wore a bright red T-shirt.

Remaema's father asked where he got such precious things.

"From the nabë," he replied.

"Brother, you are helping the nabë, who are cutting down our trees?"

8

"These people are powerful..." Moawa replied angrily. "They have guns. They can kill us before we get close enough to hit them with an arrow. If we give them what they want, they will reward us. If we don't help them, they will take it anyway."

Then everyone spoke at once and started arguing.

"STOP!"

Her grandfather's shout made Remaema jump. Everyone went quiet. "I have travelled far, and I have seen the nabë cutting down trees, destroying our world. If we help them, we make our own ruin."

Moawa defended himself. "The forest will return: we make clearings, too, for growing bananas and *casava*. When we move on, trees soon cover our gardens…"

"No!" The old man stopped him. "We make small clearings. But when the nabë come, they take away every tree. When all the trees have gone, the animals die. It is the animals that spread the seeds of the trees. No animals, no forest. No forest, no food. Then we will all starve."

Remaema's grandfather was right. To grow their plants, the farmers cut down trees and set fire to the forest.
They soon moved on, but the trees did not grow back.

The fires scared away the forest animals. Peccaries used to be common once, but after the nabë came, hunters no longer caught these tasty forest pigs. Many fruit trees had vanished, too. Finding enough food took much longer. Sometimes there was nothing at all.

The nabë needed the help of guides such as Moawa. They offered tools, clothes and money in exchange. But afterwards, the farmers only paid the guides half of what they had promised. Villagers tried to hunt down the nabë who had cheated them, but the farmers kept them away with their guns.

Then Remaema met a nabë who was not like the others.
She was washing, when the sound of a motor boat drifted
upriver. Remaema watched from the forest shadows.

A young woman began unloading.
Remaema started to creep away.

"Wait! Don't go!" To her surprise, Remaema
could understand the tall, blond woman's words.

"Take this…" The woman held out a shiny square.
It reflected Remaema's face like a puddle, only brighter.

"My name is Jane. Do you live near here? Can I meet
your family?"

"She asks a lot of questions," said Remaema's mother
later, turning the mirror in her hand. "Is this all she gave
you?" She could see that Remaema liked Jane, and she
told Remaema's father. He persuaded everyone to gather
in the yano to meet the woman.

15

Jane explained that she wanted to learn how forest people use plants to treat disease.

But an angry shout interrupted her: "You nabë are all alike! You take what you want, then disappear."

Jane's face became as red as *nara xihi* seeds. "No! I have come to save the forest and the plants and animals that live here," she said. "The people who are burning the trees do not know the value of what they are destroying.

You cannot live here without the forest. This alone is a good enough reason to protect the trees. But the forest plants and creatures you collect could help solve hunger and sick people in other parts of the world. To study them, we must save everything, for every tree or beast depends on all the others. We can't do it without your help.  You understand the forest."

Jane's speech lasted a long time. Afterwards there was a silence. Then one of the tribe's elders stood up.

"Very well," he said. "We will help you."

The forest people helped Jane with her study for half a year.

Soon after she left, Remaema's brother was playing at warriors with other boys in the garden. Throwing himself to the ground as if struck by a poisoned arrow, he shouted playfully, "Yow! I am dying, but my children will destroy your village, and kill your children…"

Then another boy fell to the ground. At first, everyone laughed. But he did not get up. He just lay among the plantain trees, covered in sweat.

"I'm s-s-so c-cold" he shivered. They carried him back to his hammock in the yano and his mother, Bahimi, asked a *shaman* to cure him.

The old healer paced around the hammock, calling on the spirits causing the illness to leave the boy's body. Afterwards, the shaman said, "He has malaria. Until we mixed with the nabë we never caught this sickness. To cure him, you need to collect bitter vine bark."

Remaema went to look for the vine bark with Bahimi. After two days walking along the shady forest trails, they neared the place where the vines grew. But something wasn't right. Smoke in the air made Remaena cough.

Half an hour later, they stepped out from the trees into brilliant sunlight. The forest was gone!  The ground was burned black as far as they could see.

Bahimi wept. Now her son would have to get better without vine bark to help him.

When at last the boy recovered, Remaema brought him flowers
and his mother painted his body with red dye.

"You are well again," she told him. "But the wounds in our village
cannot heal."

She was right. Perhaps the young men who wanted change would
have argued for ever with the tribal elders, But a few weeks later,
an Indian leader visited the village. He was famous. People spoke
his name with quiet respect: "Rikomi is coming!"

Like the villagers, Rikomi belonged to the Yanomami tribe, but he wore shoes and worked for the government in the city. Rikomi had not forgotten the battles he once fought against the nabë farmers and miners. Remaema shivered when she saw the scars on his body.

When Rikomi spoke to the grown-ups of the village, Remaema listened too.

Swinging gently in a hammock, Rikomi spoke quietly.

"There doesn't have to be a fight between tradition and progress. Not everyone outside the forest wants to destroy it."

Remaema saw her father nod.

"Some nabë love the forest. You all know about Jane, who came to study healing plants. There are also tourists who want to visit the forest because it is home to half of all the Earth's living things."

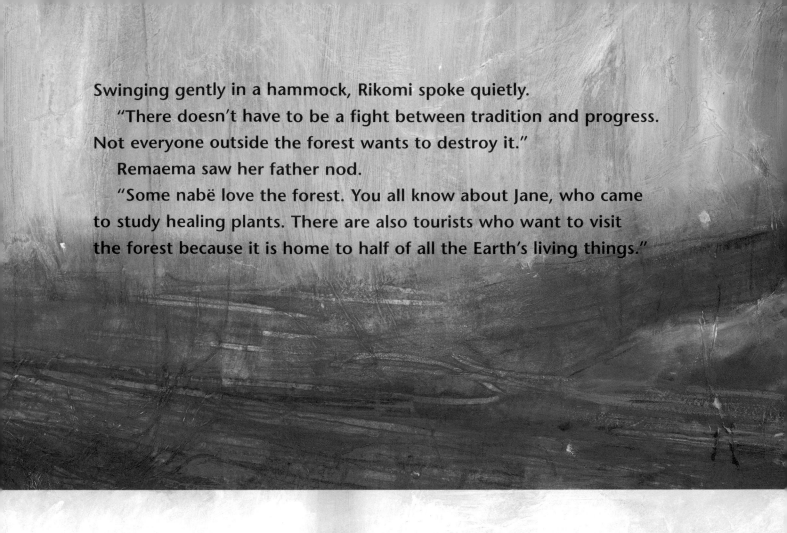

Another voice spoke. In a low chant an old warrior repeated, "My bow will kill them!"

The other villagers calmed the old man, and Rikomi went on, "Tourists could stay near the village, but not close enough to disturb life in the yano. We could show them the forest. Their money would pay for education and better health care, and for the government to keep nabë farmers away."

Eventually, everyone agreed – even Moawa.

A few months later, Remaema's uncle set off briskly
from the yano.

"Where are you going, Moawa?" asked Remaema..

"I'm off to find *yao nahi* trees for the visitors' house,"
he replied.

"But uncle, we already have plenty of logs."

"Ha! But we'll need stronger wood for the roof-beams,
and I know just where to find the trees." With that, Moawa
swaggered off into the forest, swinging his machete.

Remaema turned back into the clearing, where villagers were lifting the first posts for the new tourist hut. The project was bringing harmony back to the village.

Remaema was just thinking about this when she smelt a strong, musky odour, and heard a scuffle. That could mean only one thing. She raced back to the yano.

"Quick! Fetch your bows, everybody! The peccaries have come back!"

# WHY RAINFORESTS MATTER

Rainforests once ringed the world like a belt. They covered much of the wettest land around the Earth's middle. The forests are shrinking fast. Nearly half have gone because people cut trees wastefully for timber or to make paper. Every second, timber workers cut down an area of rainforest as big as 16 tennis courts.

Jane, the scientist in the story, knows that we must preserve the rainforest because of the huge variety of useful and beautiful plants and animals that live there. For each kind of rainforest plant that scientists have found and named, there may be as many as six more yet to be discovered. Forest people are the only ones who know how to make food or healing drugs from these plants. Some South American groups use as many as 1300 different plants.

But there is another reason for preserving the world's great rainforests. They control our planet's climate, its weather pattern. The trees soak up waste gasses that pollute the atmosphere. Cutting down the trees frees the gasses. This changes the climate, making it hotter and stormier.

By preserving the rainforests and the plants, people and other animals they contain, we are safeguarding our own health – and the health of our planet.

# GLOSSARY

*casava* (page 10): Food plant with large fleshy roots used for making flour.

*machete* (pages 8, 26): Light axe used for cutting small trees.

*nabë* (pages 6, 8, 10, 11, 13, 14, 16, 19, 23, 24): Yanomami name for white people or strangers.

*nara xihi* (page 18): Yanomami name for a forest plant collected for the bright red dye on its seeds.

*peccary* (pages 13, 27): Small, fierce, forest pig hunted for food.

*rainforest* (page 28): Dense woodland growing in some of the warmest, wettest parts of the world.

*shaman* (page 19): Healer-priest who talks to ghosts and gods, following their advice to cure ills and perform magic.

*yano* (pages 8, 15, 24, 26, 27): Yanomami word for a large, circular forest shelter where many families live together.

*Yanomami tribe*: The people in this book – a Native South American people who live in the rainforests of south Venezuela and north Brazil.

*yao nahi* (page 26): Forest tree with a very strong trunk, used for building.

# MORE TITLES FROM FRANCES LINCOLN CHILDREN'S BOOKS

## B is for Brazil
Maria de Fatima Campos

From Carnival to Guarana, from Football to Zebu,
here is a celebration of Brazil in all its cultural diversity.

ISBN 978-1-84507-316-9

## 101 Ways to Save the Earth
David Bellamy
Illustrated by Penny Dann

Facts and tips on how to live an ecologically-sound
life and conserve the planet in the process!

ISBN 978-0-7112-2161-1 (UK)

## The Drop in My Drink –
## The Story of Water on our Planet
Meredith Hooper
Illustrated by Chris Coady

The intriguing story of a drop of water, from the
beginnings of our planet to the water cycle of today.

ISBN 978-1-84507-837-9

Frances Lincoln titles are available from all good bookshops.
You can also buy books and find out more about your favourite titles,
authors and illustrators on our website: www.franceslincoln.com.

modification of actions that have remained essentially biologic among all other creatures.

While archeologists can discover a great deal about past forms of material culture, they are prevented by the very nature of their methods and aims from learning much that is essential for an understanding of the workings of biocultural behavior. To find out more about this central aspect of human life it was necessary to turn to the findings of cultural anthropologists. After many facts had been gathered from primitive societies throughout the world, comparative ethnological analyses revealed that beneath a bewildering profusion of differing details a kind of universal pattern could be discerned. In the course of time it was found that most of the features of each society's design for group living fell into a configuration whose minimum essentials could be expressed as a triangle. It was also found that the various segments of the triangle were closely interrelated and that the entire figure might be said to have a distinctive slant or emphasis. With this doctrine as a common base, contemporary cultural anthropologists have branched out in various ways. A number continue to visit primitive societies yet unknown to science and to describe their patterns of culture; some concentrate on the tasks of studying how cultural configurations are held together or changed; many try to find out how ways of life are taught and learned; others look into the consequences which demands for conformity to cultural values have on the personalities of individuals; and still others have begun to transfer ethnological techniques from the investigation of small, homogeneous, primitive tribes to large, heterogeneous, literate societies such as are commonly found in the Western World. Increased understanding of the nature of man, society, and culture has resulted from the combined efforts of all these investigators.

## D. LOOKING FORWARD

An anthropologist would be unfaithful to his convictions if he feared to look ahead and make predictions. For all that has already been accomplished in the science of man, much more remains to be done. If the cultural activities of *Homo sapiens* are to be directed to socially desirable goals for all mankind, human behavior must be brought into the range of controlled causation. Before this can be done, greater knowledge will have to be obtained in several critical areas.

Future research will have to be directed in part, at least, to the problem of cultural origins. If it be true that man alone is capable of symbolic behavior, what is there in his biophysicochemical composition that sets him apart from all other animals? At the moment we are forced to postulate that algebraic mentality is somehow a function of increased brain size. If that is so, what is the precise threshold below which symbolization is impossible? If other factors are involved, what are they and how do they function? And when the matter of origins has been settled, we would still like to know exactly why so many cultural values apparently run counter to biological necessities. Why should people everywhere, in varying degree, make efforts to conceal activities involving excretion or sexual relations? Why should an American who has dined well feel ashamed if someone tells him that he has crumbs on his lips? Why do members of many societies feel uneasy about eating in full view of others? It is simple enough to rationalize some of these attitudes, as by postulating that the odors of stale urine or fresh feces are offensive, but there is no universal agreement on what constitutes a bad smell, and numerous tribes are indifferent about handling the waste products of the human body. Navaho young women show no noticeable distaste when scraping fecal material from garments, yet they do not defecate in their living quarters; and in recent years Hopi men drank urine as medicine and used it for fixing dyes, but never did they urinate indoors after infancy.

Suppose we bypass the question of origins and simply assume that all normal humans have the capacity to symbolize, and that all societies formulate biocultural standards for living together. We are then faced with a new set of questions which future investigators must try to answer. How does a configuration of culture acquire an emphasis, conveniently called Dionysian or Apollonian, which nearly resembles the personality structures of certain kinds of individuals? What is the exact nature of the process of interiorization? What happens to a child's inherited structure as it learns to conform to the cultural values of its society? In other words, what price does an individual pay for adjusting to biocultural norms, particularly if they run counter to his inborn biology? Then again, other basic problems await solution in respect to many facets of individual and group behavior. What is the process by which a society arrives at a decision or expresses a preference? How do systems of values arise and change? What is the difference between reaching a social decision and an individual decision? Why are some aspects of a foreign culture eagerly accepted while others are stubbornly resisted? Why are people more willing to develop the new motor habits required for the use of borrowed material objects than they are to acquire new forms of speech? More basic still would be satisfactory answers to the questions of why mankind in general has made cultural rather than biological adjustments and why the species has so consistently favored the saving of time and the conservation of human muscular energy. Partial explanations for some of these matters are already available, but a great deal that is now uncertain will have to be clarified by future research workers.

An area that is badly in need of new approaches and further work is the field of **cultural dynamics.** We know that there are forces making for stabilization and equilibrium and others that bring about disruption, change, or disintegration, but when it comes to understanding the nature of these forces, social scientists are almost as badly off as were students of organic evolution before there was any knowledge of genetics. Every person as well as every social unit is continuously subject to the pressure of shifting sociocultural forces. We take it for granted that an individual must be prepared to live by varying sets of cultural values as he grows from infancy to old age or enters on different marital or occupational statuses; and now that isolation is virtually impossible, we expect whole societies to be ever ready to confront the possibility of change. Yet, we cannot claim to know how to control these processes, because we know pitifully little about how they work.

Anthropologists of the future may also have to concern themselves with still another aspect of dynamics, the relations of cultural to biological forces. Both of these may be seen operating in the field of man's interplay with his physical environment. The needs for oxygen, food, drink, and shelter from the elements originate as biological imperatives, but since man cannot satisfy them with the attributes of his own body, the biological needs stimulate cultural responses and so serve as forces of culture. These forces press upon every society that seeks to survive and express themselves in the form of particular cultural adjustments or institutions. Too many contemporary social scientists are concerned with institutions and pay scant attention to the forces that bring them into being. It is a little like trying to understand the working of electric light bulbs without knowing anything about electricity. Man's relations to man likewise consist of institutions, such as marriage or child-raising, that may be interpreted as cultural responses to biological forces; but for the present, man's dealings with the supernatural can seldom be directly connected with his biology, and must be attributed largely to socio-cultural pressures. Once cultural anthropologists begin to deal with basic forces rather than institutions, they may find themselves in a better position to formulate scientific laws on the basis of which sound predictions can be made.

## E. CONCLUSION

There are many reasons why a book of this kind should end on a note of optimism. Modern anthropology is only a century old, has attempted to cover a diversified range of topics, and has dealt with a tremendously long span of time, but it has received professional attention from a relatively small number of scholars. Nevertheless, it has aroused great interest and has had a valuable stimulating effect on other disciplines devoted to an understanding of man. Above all, cultural anthropologists have proved that it is possible for human beings to study their fellow men dispassionately and have shown that no generalizations about mankind are valid unless the entire species is taken into account. No longer can a few men and women of a single type, from a single region, or possessed of a single way of life be regarded as the equivalent of *Homo sapiens.*

The anthropological view of man has served to call into question the claims of all those who would glorify one stock or race at the expense of another. Biological differences among various groups of mankind have been more closely investigated by physical anthropologists than by any other scientists, and their conclusions are soundly based and positive. No race is biologically better than any other; mixture between stocks or races is not biologically harmful; there are no sure differences of mental potential; no society of humans lives on a purely "animal" level; and any group of mankind has the capacity to learn any other unit's patterns of biocultural behavior.

In the study of man's behavior, anthropologists have also made outstanding contributions. Through the painstaking work of archeologists, they have been able to show the great antiquity of human efforts to develop culture, the various stages through which it has passed, and the different combinations of traits that have developed in various localities. At the same time they have provided evidence of the existence of universal laws of culture growth whose operations override regional considerations. What archeologists dealing with extinct peoples and cultures could not do, cultural anthropologists have undertaken. They have shown how human beings as living organisms interact with all phases of their cultures, and they have worked out the basic configurations that patterned ways of life seem to take in all societies.

Finally, some aspects of cultural anthropology deserve special mention. Field workers have shown that ways of life must be studied as wholes, wherein each part is not only integrated with the others, but is also affected by them. Furthermore, they have refused to measure primitive cultures against any preconceived notions of right and wrong, good and bad. There was a time when the anthropological insistence on cultural relativism threatened to do away with absolute concepts such as normality for all humans; but quite recently, on the basis of wider knowledge of universal forms of behavior, new absolute standards are being formulated. As a last word, anthropologists have found no barriers, in theory, to the establishment of a pattern of culture for human beings everywhere. There is a noteworthy trend nowadays for small social groups to amalgamate into larger units. Should this trend continue indefinitely it will lead to the formation of a universal society, and whenever the peoples of the world may require it, cultural anthropologists will be found ready to help fashion a diversified way of life that will suit the needs of all mankind.

## SELECTED REFERENCES

Chapple, E. D., "Applied Anthropology in Industry," *Anthropology Today*, A. L. Kroeber, ed., pp. 819-831. Chicago, 1953.

———, and Arensberg, C. M., "Measuring Human Relations: An Introduction to the Study of the Interaction of Individuals," *Genetic Psychology Monographs*, No. 22, 1940.

Datta-Majumdar, N., *The Santal: A Study in Culture Change*. Delhi, India, 1956.

Hollingshead, A. de B., *Elmtown's Youth, the Impact of Social Classes on Adolescents*. New York, 1949.

Leighton, A. H., *The Governing of Men*. Princeton, N. J., 1946.

Lynd, R. S., and H. M., *Middletown: A Study of American Culture*. New York, 1929.

———, *Middletown in Transition*. New York, 1937.

Miner, H. M., "The Folk-Urban Continuum," *American Sociological Review*, Vol. 17, No. 5, 1952, pp. 529-537.

Redfield, R., *The Folk Culture of Yucatan*. Chicago, 1942.

Roethlisberger, F. J., and Dickson, W. J., *Management and the Worker*. Boston, 1934.

Seeley, R., *et al.*, *Crestwood Heights: A Study of Suburban Life*. New York, 1956.

Titiev, M., "Araucanian Culture in Transition," *Occasional Contributions from the Museum of Anthropology*, No. 15, Ann Arbor, Mich., 1951.

Warner, W. L., *et al.*, *Yankee City Series*. New Haven, 1941 ff.

West, J., *Plainville, U. S. A*. New York, 1945.

# GLOSSARY [1]

Reference to pages where the terms defined occur will be found in the Index.

**Abbevillian** A stage of Western Europe's culture. See **Paleolithic Age.**

**acculturation** The process of intermingling of cultural elements, in part or on the whole. May result from the impact of a Euro-American group on a primitive society, but may also come about in other ways.

**Acheulian** A stage of Western Europe's culture. See **Paleolithic Age.**

**achieved status** The social standing acquired by effort. See **ascribed status.**

**action anthropology** A branch of applied anthropology which aims to improve native conditions in terms of goals set by the natives themselves.

**aerophones** Musical instruments that produced tones by the vibration of closed columns of air, as in flutes and Panpipes.

**affinal** Relationship established by marriage, as opposed to **natal** or **consanguineal** relationships.

**age-group** A class or set of persons, ordinarily of the same sex, who are of approximately the same age. Where they are recognized to form a unit, they may be expected to cooperate in carrying out particular duties.

**algebraic mentality** The ability to assign or change non-sensory meanings or values ascribed to anything that is used as a symbol. This capacity seems limited to human beings with large, healthy **Primate** brains.

**alloy** A fusion of two or more metals forming a substance with properties of its own.

**alternate generation harmony** The agreeable relations that frequently prevail between members of every second generation, such as those between grandparents and grandchildren.

**amniote egg** Egg in which a thin membrane forms a sac enwrapping an embryo; the type from which an offspring develops in reptiles, birds, and mammals.

**amulet** Any object, usually worn by a person, to which supernatural power has been ascribed; commonly used as a defense against evil forces.

**animatism** Belief that inanimate or inorganic things may contain supernatural power.

**animism** The doctrine that all living things contain a supernatural element widely equated with the life principle, or soul.

**Apollonian** Descriptive of an individual whose temperament is shy and restrained, or else of a social group in which qualities such as self-control or sobriety are esteemed.

---

[1] Thanks are due my son, Bob, who helped me prepare the glossary and index.

**arch** See **corbeled arch** and **true arch.**

**Archanthropinae** The most ancient forms of extinct hominids, greatly different from *Homo sapiens,* that have ever been recovered, including *Pithecanthropus erectus* and *Sinanthropus pekinensis.* Most belong to the early Pleistocene Age.

**archeology** An important branch of general anthropology. Its practioners discover, excavate where necessary, and interpret the remains of former cultures.

**articulate speech** Speech that consists of the utterance of clearly distinct and distinguishable units of sound.

**artifact** Any object that is consciously manufactured for human use.

**ascribed status** That standing in a social structure that a person holds simply by virtue of birth, proper sex, or age.

**associations** Social groups voluntarily formed or entered for some special purpose. In primitive societies they generally balance clusters of individuals linked together by involuntary bonds of relationship.

**Aurignacian** A stage of Western Europe's culture. See **Paleolithic Age.**

**Australopithecinae** A general term for the whole group of extinct man-apes recently discovered in South Africa.

**avoidance** Term for the socioculturally prescribed avoidance of some people by certain others.

**basic personality type** The kind of temperament or personality type that is most common among the members of a given social unit. Believed to arise when people are subjected to similar sociocultural forces or **institutions.**

**berdache** A man who dresses and acts like a woman. Not all berdaches are real transvestites or homosexuals.

**biocultural unconformity** The situation that develops whenever a person is subjected at one and the same time to a conflict between biological and cultural forces, motivations, expressions, values, or objectives. Such situations are always potentially dangerous.

**biological imperatives** The essential activities or commands which every living organism must carry out if it is to maintain its life and reproduce its kind.

**blade** A parallel-sided, somewhat rectangular, blank or tool of flint, usually made from a previously prepared core. Blade implements were commonly used only in the later or upper phases of the **Paleolithic Age.**

**botanical animism** The belief that all things in the plant kingdom have a vital principle, life force, or soul, often equated with **mana.**

**brachiating** The method of progression whereby a creature swings by the hands and arms. Usually associated with tree life and best exemplified by gibbons and some species of American monkeys.

**brachycephalic** Broad-headed. A skull or head which is at least 80 percent as broad as it is long.

**butterfly-wings** Hairdress consisting of large circular loops of hair worn above the ears. Among the Hopi Indians, worn only by unmarried women.

**calendrical rites** Supernatural ceremonies scheduled in advance to be performed at certain times or seasons. They must be socially desirable as they take no account of individual wants.

**caste** A group of persons, marked by a particular occupation, who are expected to marry only among themselves. Castes are usually hereditary, and have a fixed status in a social hierarchy.

**casting** The pouring of molten metal into a heat-resistant form, so that it will take the shape of the form when it cools and hardens.

**cell** A unit of **protoplasm** consisting, in most cases, of a **nucleus** containing **genes** arranged in **chromosomes,** and surrounding material loosely called cytoplasm.

**celt** A polished stone tool, resembling a modern hatchet blade or ax-head. It was always attached to a handle and was widely used in the **Neolithic** Age.

**cephalic index** A device used in classifying subdivisions of *Homo sapiens.* It expresses as a percentage the width of a person's head or skull in proportion to its length. The higher the cephalic index, the more broad-headed the person.

**cerebral cortex** That portion of the gray matter of the brain that overlies the front hemisphere, or cerebrum.

**cerebrotonic** Dr. W. H. Sheldon's term to describe people who are guided by thought. According to Sheldon, cerebrotonic individuals are usually tall and thin **(ectomorphic).**

**ceremonial coyness** Socioculturally prescribed reluctance to take an action, may or may not express an individual's true feelings, and is often expected to be shown by a bride.

**charm** An object thought to contain supernatural power; customarily worn to attract favorable forces.

**Chellian** A stage of Western Europe's culture. See **Paleolithic Age.**

**chordophones** Musical instruments, like violins, that produce tones by the vibrations of strings.

**chromosome** Ordinarily taken to be like a tiny string of **genes.** Wherever reproduction is bisexual, each parent is believed to contribute one of every pair of chromosomes that is contained in the nuclei of **cells.**

**cire-perdue** A method for manufacturing metallic objects by fitting clay over a wax model. When heated, the wax runs out and is replaced by molten metal.

**clan** A **unilateral** cluster of relatives, following along one sex line only, who are held together by the shared belief that they are descended from a common ancestor. Common in primitive societies, where it may have social, political, economic, artistic, and religious functions.

**class** As opposed to a **caste,** a class refers to a group of persons who have the same social status but who can move from class to class in keeping with their attainments.

**classificatory** A method of labeling kindred whereby a number of persons may share one term. Thus an individual may have a number of fathers, mothers, and so forth. This supports the contention that a kinship system is a sociocultural rather than a genetic phenomenon.

**clavicle** The collar bone. An important feature of Primate anatomy, it makes possible strenuous movements of the arms and hands to the sides and rear of the body.

**clitoridectomy** An operation on the clitoris performed in some primitive societies.

**consanguineous** Descriptive of a relationship based on supposed ties of common blood, or **genes.**

**contagious** Used, most often, in the phrase "contagious magic" to describe certain supernatural beliefs or practices. It refers to the flow or movement of power as the result of contact.

**corbeled arch** A false arch constructed by having two sides, each built by a series of overlaps, meet at a central point.

**council of elders** A form of political control, **gerontocracy,** in which authority is vested in a group of oldsters.

**counting coup** In several Plains Indian tribes, a systematic and carefully graded scheme for winning honors in war. Greatest prestige of all went to a warrior who touched an unwounded enemy. Claims had to be supported by oaths or witnesses.

**couvade** The practice of having husbands lie in, after their wives have given birth. In extreme form, found among several Amazonian tribes, men may mimic the pain and process of childbirth.

**cranial capacity** A measure of gross brain size expressed in cubic centimeters.

**critical points** Basic to the concept that marked qualitative changes occur only at certain critical points or **thresholds** along a numerical continuum. Except where reversible reactions are concerned, it is practically never possible to revert exactly to an earlier stage after a threshold has been passed.

**critical rites** Practices, based on a belief in the supernatural, designed to help an individual or a society in time of crisis.

**critical thresholds** See **critical points.**

**Cro-Magnon** A type of **hominid** closely resembling modern man, dominant in Western Europe during the later Pleistocene period.

**cross-cousin marriage** Union between the offspring of a brother and those of his sister. This kind of marriage is often preferred or prescribed in primitive societies. Among other things, it has the effect of making children take mates from the same natal **household group** as did the parent of their sex, of making brothers and sisters the parents-in-law of one another's offspring, and, later, of making a brother and his sister the grandparents of the same youngsters.

**cross-cousins** The children of a man and those of his sister.

**Crow kinship system** A method of naming relatives which has separate terms for mother's sister and father's sister, but which puts under the same label a woman and her feminine descendants through females, regardless of generation lines.

**cultural anthropology** That branch of anthropology which specializes in studying the ways of life that prevail among all the living individuals who constitute a society. In the United States, it often overlaps, and is sometimes interchangeable with, **ethnology, social anthropology,** and **ethnography.**

**cultural blindness** A convenient phrase for a custom whereby an individual fails to note something glimpsed, which he regards as unimportant or which his society thinks he ought not to have seen.

**cultural configurations** The patterns into which the prescribed and repetitive ways of life of any society seem to fall. All the parts of such configurations are closely linked together.

**cultural dynamics** Study of the interacting and changing forces, sometimes conflicting, that a pattern of culture must keep in balance in order to preserve its equilibrium and prevent itself from disintegrating.

**culture** The complete range of objects, values, symbolic meanings, and repetitive ways of behaving that guide the conduct of individual members of a society. No aspect of culture can be biogenetically transmitted, and each person must learn postnatally the features of culture that pertain to him. Patterns, or configurations, of culture may persist beyond the deaths of particular individuals.

**culture area** A region or territorial zone within which one way of life is predominant. There is usually a noticeable difference in important aspects between one culture area and another.

**cuneiform** A form of writing, employing wedge-shaped characters, that was used in many parts of the Near East during the Bronze Age.

**descriptive** A method of labeling kindred that is supposed, theoretically, to use a single term for each type of relationship. In practice, as our term "cousin" indicates, one term may cover a variety of relationships.

**diffusion** The spread of a cultural item from its place of origin to other places. Thus, the opposite of local, or **independent, invention.**

**Dionysian** Descriptive of a person of outgoing and aggressive temperament, or else of a society whose members esteem daring, unrestrained, intemperate, and reckless behavior.

**divination** The act of finding out or foretelling the wishes or designs of supernatural powers. May also refer to methods of discovering hidden information, such as the whereabouts of lost objects.

**dolichocephalic** Long-headed. A skull or head the breadth of which is less than 75 percent of its length. See **cephalic index.**

**double descent** The system of having two different **unilateral** groups of kindred in one society, as, for example, both a mother's and a father's units.

**dysphoria** A general feeling of unrest, unhappiness, uneasiness, or dissatisfaction; tends to prevail throughout a society when its culture is disintegrating or changing quickly.

**ectomorphic** A term used to designate tall, thin individuals who have a great deal of skin, nerve, and brain area in relation to volume.

**Ego** Usually a hypothetical, adult male, from whose viewpoint a kinship system is customarily presented.

**emancipation of the forelimbs** A phrase used to describe the anatomical freeing of the front appendages from any duties connected with the support or movement of the body.

**enculturation** The universal process whereby every human baby learns from birth on to adjust its behavior to the **culture** of its society.

**endogamy** The custom whereby approved marriages must always take place within the bounds of particular social units; generally contrasted with **exogamy.**

**endomorphic** Descriptive of a person with a soft, rounded body, usually having a great deal of fat in the abdominal region.

**eolith** A natural stone utilized as a tool, without having been consciously manufactured. Some people claim that the earliest of men must have used unworked stones, recognizable by the markings resulting from usage.

**Ertebølle** A stage of **Mesolithic** culture in Scandinavia, featuring **kitchen middens.**

**ethnocentric** Culture-bound, tending to interpret the cultures of other people in terms of one's own way of life. Ethnocentricism usually implies a tendency to regard as "bad" any deviations from one's own pattern of culture.

**ethnography** The description of ways of life. See **cultural anthropology.**

**ethnology** In the United States this term refers to the study and analysis of ways of life. It has the implication of giving greater attention to theory than does **ethnography.** See **cultural anthropology.**

**ethnomusicology** The comparative study of music in all societies, including primitive ones.

**Eutherian mammals** That subclass of mammals whose females nourish their young during pregnancy by means of a deciduous **placenta.**

**exogamy** A social requirement that approved marriages must take place outside certain units of society. As in **endogamy,** it is the total society that determines what those units shall be.

**false arch** See **corbeled arch.**

**family of orientation** The family group within which a newly born child learns about its culture.

**family of procreation** The family group in which a married **Ego** begets and rears children.

**fetish** Any inanimate object to which a society ascribes supernatural power.

**fetusphilic** A term used to describe a society whose members treat a **neonate** tenderly by trying to reproduce conditions to which it had become accustomed in its mother's womb.

**fetusphobic** A term used to describe a society whose members treat a **neonate** harshly, as by bathing it in cold water.

**fibula** Anatomically, the larger of the two long bones that run from ankle to knee in man. Archeologically, a safety-pin from the Copper-Bronze or Iron Ages.

**first-fruit rites** Usually, these are harvest rituals, during which part of the first yield is dedicated as a thanksgiving offering to the divinities thought responsible for enabling a society to obtain food. May be applied to the first seasonal appearance of any kind of food.

**folklore** Popular, anonymous tales, often told among nonliterate or illiterate people.

**folk society** A peasant-like community. May be only a backward portion of a highly modern nation.

**foramen magnum** The major opening at the base of a **Primate** skull or head, through which the top of the spinal column enters.

**forging** In **metallurgy**, the forming of an object by repeated heating and hammering.

**Freud, Sigmund** The great psychologist whose insights founded psychoanalysis and laid much of the modern basis for the investigation of mental processes.

**geisha** Professional female entertainers in traditional Japan; they were not the same as prostitutes. Often hired by men for private parties.

**genes** Tiny biochemical particles supposed to be the units of biogenetic heredity. Most scientists think of them as component parts of **chromosomes.**

**genna tabu** A period of time, often following the death of an important personage, when it is forbidden to undertake any but the most essential of actions.

**genotype** An organism whose form, or any of its parts, is thought to result only from the workings of its intrinsic genetic or hereditary material.

**gerontocracy** See **council of elders.**

**glottochronology** A technique for determining the time when separated speakers of related languages first moved apart. Also called **lexicostatistics.**

**grinding** See **polishing.**

**hafting** Increasing the mechanical efficiency of a tool by affixing it to a handle. First employed during the **Mousterian** phase of the **Paleolithic Age.**

**hemoglobin** The red coloring matter of the corpuscles that carry oxygen in the bloodstream.

**heterodont** Having teeth that vary in shape, size, and function.

**heterosis** The phenomenon of **hybrid vigor,** whereby the offspring of differing parents exhibit a tendency to gain in size and strength.

**hieroglyphic** A form of writing by arranging pictorial symbols in rows or columns.

**hominid** Manlike or mannish. Any creature whose anatomical structure closely approximates that of *Homo sapiens.*

**homodont** Having teeth that are all alike.

**household group** As a unit of kindred, this term applies to all relatives in one sex line of descent, who customarily share a common residence.

**hybrid vigor** See **heterosis.**

**idiophones** Musical instruments, including rattles or gongs, that create tones by the setting up of vibrations within the entire implement.

**idol** A carving, usually three-dimensional, to which supernatural power is ascribed; often supposed to depict the appearance of the associated supernatural power.

**imitation magic** See **mimetic magic.**

**incest** Prohibited sexual relations between certain kin. Practically universal are tabus on relations between parents and offspring, and between brothers and sisters; but societies may forbid mating on many grounds other than consanguinity.

**independent invention** Any invention which is developed in a given locality and not borrowed from an outside source. It thus affords a contrast to **diffusion.**

**initiation by trespass** The enforced initiation of anyone who has trespassed on a spot where a society was conducting a closed, secret ritual.

**institutions** As used in this book, the term denotes socially approved and standardized or repetitive responses to sociocultural forces.

**javelin-thrower** See **spear-thrower.**

**joking relationships** Socially approved and usually standardized forms of familiarity that are expected to prevail between certain types of relatives.

**kachinas** Male dancers who become gods or spirits among the Hopi and other Pueblo tribes as soon as they don masks. Kachinas sing as they dance; simple membership in their cult is tribalwide and open to members of both sexes.

**kinship sets** Clusters comprising kindred bound together by one or more ties of relationship.

**kitchen middens** Heaps or mounds of debris that often accumulate near human settlements. When excavated by trained archeologists, they may yield information about extinct cultures. See **Ertebølle.**

**kiva** A subterranean religious chamber, sometimes used by men only for social purposes, that is typically found in the villages of the Pueblo Indians.

**kris** A short sword or dagger customarily worn by men in Malaysia.

**La Chapelle-aux-Saints** Place in France where the most widely described specimen of **Neandertal man** was found.

**law of controlled causation** A law of cultural evolution which states that as any problem comes under the certain control of a society, it is no longer left for solution to a supernatural agency. As an increase of knowledge brings more and more things within a society's control, it has the effect of reducing the society's reliance on the supernatural.

**legend** A folk tale in which the principal characters and events are historical or pseudohistorical. On this account, legends are sometimes differentiated from **myths,** which are frankly supernatural, but the distinction is not always clear.

**Levallois** **Lower Paleolithic** technique for the manufacture of stone tools from flakes.

**levirate** The custom that entitles a widow to marry one of her late husband's brothers. Note that it does not entail arrangements with a new **household group.**

**lexicostatistics** See **glottochronology.**

**lineage** A **unilateral** line of **consanguineous** kindred, whom a society believes to be closely and demonstrably related by virtue of descent from a common ancestor or ancestress.

**loess** Fine particles of loam or fertile soil commonly blown out of a dry area by winds, but sometimes borne by water.

**lost-wax** See **cire-perdue.**

**Magdalenian** A stage of Western Europe's culture. See **Paleolithic Age.**

**magic** Rituals involving a belief in the supernatural, performed for the benefit of those who request them. Magicians tend to work by formulas that compel supernatural agencies to do their bidding if the formulas are properly executed. Most cultural anthropologists feel that there is a subtle distinction between magic and religion, but some scholars treat them as one. Magical rites are **critical** and are virtually never **calendrical.**

**Maglemose** A **Mesolithic** culture of Europe, which flourished along the Baltic Sea.

**malleable** Capable of being beaten into sheets, an important property of many metals.

**mana** A general term for supernatural power. The word was first noted in Melanesia, but it is now used by cultural anthropologists who study supernaturalism anywhere in the world.

**mantic "sciences"** "Sciences" of prophecy, usually based on a determination by man of supernatural plans for the future. See **divination.**

**marital frigidity** The inability of a spouse, most often a wife, to enjoy sexual relations with a legal mate.

**matrilineal** Reckoning descent unilaterally only through one's mother. By this means, a **unilateral** descent group is formed by a woman and the offspring of her female descendants.

**matrilocal** A postmarital residence rule that requires a groom to live in or near his bride's natal household.

**medicine man** See **shaman.**

**membraphones** Musical instruments, such as drums, that produce tones by the vibration of a membrane.

**mesocephalic** Medium-headed. Heads or skulls which are 75 to 80 percent as broad as they are long.

**Mesolithic** That phase of cultural evolution that falls between the **Paleolithic** and the **Neolithic.** May refer either to the tools and other objects that were then current or to the time involved. For most of the Old World this would mean approximately from 20,000 to 6,000 B.C. Some anthropologists regard the Mesolithic as a mere extension of the **Upper Paleolithic.**

**mesomorphic** Descriptive of an individual whose skeletal frame is sturdy and rugged and whose muscles are powerful.

**metallurgy** Any technique for dealing with superheated or molten metals.

**Metazoa** Animals or plants whose bodies consist of multiple cells.

**microlith** An implement fashioned by man from a tiny bit of stone.

**mimetic magic** Efforts to influence supernatural powers to help the members of a society get what they desire by showing what is wanted. Thus, if more heat from the sun is desired, a fire might be built as part of a ceremony.

**modal personality type** See **basic personality type.**

**moiety** Each subdivision of a society that is divided into halves.

**molding** See **casting.**

**morpheme** The smallest unit of speech to which meaning is ordinarily attached.

**mother-in-law tabu** A sociocultural rule that forbids a man to look upon or converse with his mother-in-law. See **avoidance.**

**motor habits** Movements of the body or any of its parts in accord with cultural conventions. Motor habits are usually much the same for all persons of the same sex and age who occupy equivalent positions in a society.

**Mousterian** The middle phase of Paleolithic culture in Western Europe, closely associated with **Neandertal man.** See **Paleolithic Age.**

**multilocal household** A social unit comprised of unilateral kin who would presumably have shared a common residence under earlier conditions, but who now occupy two or more houses.

**myth** A folk tale in which the central figures or events are supernatural. See **legend.**

**natal kin** Relatives automatically and involuntarily acquired by an infant at birth.

**national character** The kind of personality structure that is believed to be most typical of an entire nation. See **basic personality type.**

**Neanderthal man** A type of extinct **hominid,** linked to **Mousterian** culture, that lived through the middle phases of the Pleistocene. Those in Western Europe had low skull vaults, outthrust faces, relatively chinless lower jaws, and short, thick necks.

**Neoanthropinae** A category of extinct Pleistocene **hominids** whose anatomical structures closely resembled those of *Homo sapiens.* **Cro-Magnon** types are the best known of the Neoanthropinae.

**Neolithic Age** The New Stone Age, usually considered to have begun in the Near East about 6000 B.C. It is characterized by people who lived in permanent settlements, practiced agriculture, made polished stone tools, domesticated animals, fashioned pottery, and knew how to weave.

**neolocal** A postmarital residence custom that results in newlyweds living where they please, in new homes that are not necessarily near their kin.

**neonate** A newly-born infant.

**neopallium** An organ of the brain that first appeared in reptiles and corresponds to the **cerebral cortex.**

**new-fire rites** Ceremonies that involve the kindling of fresh blazes. North of the equator such rites are generally **calendrical** and occur late in December, at the time of the winter solstice. The new-fire is usually a bit of **mimetic magic,** designed to strengthen the power of the sun, and also to convey the implication of a fresh start, such as the beginning of a new year.

**night soil** Human excrement collected nightly and widely used as fertilizer throughout the Far East.

**nuchal musculature** Muscles at the back of the neck.

**nucleus of a cell** The portion of a **cell** which contains the **genes** arranged in **chromosomes** that seem to be the agents of reproduction and the bearers of biogenetically transmitted traits of heredity.

**Omaha kinship system** The method of naming relatives, widely found in patrilineal societies, that has separate terms for father's brother and mother's brother, but which uses a single term to designate, regardless of generation, a man and all his masculine descendants through males.

**opposable thumb** A **Primate** anatomical mechanism, whereby the ball of the thumb can be opposed to the balls of the other four fingers of each hand, making possible a **prehensile grip.**

**ordeal** A test situation prepared by men, but the outcome of which is determined, theoretically, by a supernatural power that is always fair, accurate, omniscient, and neutral. In primitive societies ordeals are widely used for determinations of guilt or innocence. Harm, as a consequence of submitting to an ordeal, is believed to come only to the guilty.

**orthograde** Carriage of the body in an upright position. Among **Primates** man is the only creature that habitually carries the body upright, firmly supported on the hind legs.

**Paleoanthropinae** The forms of extinct hominids that fall between the **Archanthropinae** and the **Neoanthropinae** in the degree of their resemblance to *Homo sapiens.* Most of them lived in the more recent half of the Pleistocene. They have their greatest representation in **Neandertal man.**

**Paleolithic Age** The Old Stone Age. Represents the time and type of man's earliest, clearly recognizable forms of culture. In Western Europe it is conventionally arranged into the following subdivisions, during all of which man made stone tools by percussion or pressure, and failed to develop permanent settlements and methods of controlled food production:

A. **Lower Paleolithic**
   1. **Chellian (Abbevillian)**
   2. **Acheulian**, including the **Levallois** technique.
B. **Middle Paleolithic**
   1. **Mousterian**
C. **Upper Paleolithic**
   1. **Aurignacian**
   2. **Solutrian**
   3. **Magdalenian**

**palstave** A metal celt in which the sides rise up and meet to form an enclosed socket. Some have a ring for tying, in addition to wedging, a handle into the socket. Widespread in the Copper-Bronze Age.

**parallel cousins** The children of two brothers or of two sisters. In some societies, parallel cousins are forbidden to wed.

**participant-observer** A technique widely used by cultural anthropologists for gathering data in the field. As a rule it means that a masculine observer participates in the activities of the men he is studying, while a feminine field worker shares in the lives of the women.

**patrilineal** A **unilateral** group of kindred who trace their descent in the male line.

**phenotype** An organism, or any of its parts, whose form is presumed to result from the interplay of its inherited genetic material and such external forces as environment.

**phoneme** The smallest identifiable or contrastive unit of sound that can be distinguished in any human language.

**phonetic alphabet** A series of written letters or characters, each of which stands for a speech sound.

**phratry** In primitive societies, this is most commonly an unnamed **exogamic** unit, containing two or more **clans.** Authorities differ on whether phratries were formed by the segmentation of an original clan or by the amalgamation of originally distinct clans.

**physical anthropology** In America, that branch of general anthropology whose practitioners are concerned with all possible manifestations of the human body.

**Pithecanthropus erectus** Also known as Java man, and less widely as Trinil man. Found at Trinil, Java, by Dr. Eugene Dubois. Represents an extremely early and archaic form of extinct **hominid.**

**placenta** The internal tubes and organs by which a pregnant female in the Eutherian subclass of mammals shelters, feeds, and cleans an embryo. Discharged as the afterbirth soon after a baby has emerged from its mother's body.

**polishing** The technique most widely used in the **Neolithic Age** for the manufacture of stone tools. Called for rubbing or grinding a tool to shape by moving it back and forth across a rough, abrasive material. The resulting tool is highly polished, and smooth to the touch.

**polyandry** A custom, quite rare throughout the world, which permits one woman to have two or more husbands at the same time.

**polygamy** Any form of having, simultaneously, multiple spouses.

**polygyny** The most widespread form of multiple mating, wherein one man takes two or more wives.

**prehensile grip** The tight hand hold that a **Primate** can get by virtue of the fact that the big finger wraps around an object or tool in the opposite direction from the other four fingers. See **opposable thumb.**

**Primate** That order of **Eutherian mammals** to which belong lemurs, tarsiers, monkeys, apes, and men.

**prognathism** Protrusion of the face and jaws. Sometimes restricted to protrusion of the tooth-bearing portions of the jaws.

**projective tests** Psychological tests designed to have a subject project his personality from possibly hidden levels into the open. Tests may reveal to a trained psychologist much that has no meaning to the subject himself.

**protein** A complex combination of amino acids with carbon, hydrogen, oxygen, nitrogen, and traces of other elements. Forms the basis of **protoplasm,** or living matter.

**protoplasm** Living matter, making up the bodies of all plants and animals. Always divided into units or **cells.**

**Protozoan** A tiny animal, whose entire body consists of one **cell** of **protoplasm.**

**quipu** A knotted string used in aboriginal Peru as a reminding device. By means of various colors and knots, the Inca were capable of keeping track of complicated statistical data. Not a form of true writing.

**race** As used by anthropologists, a race is a subdivision of *Homo sapiens.* In this text the term is used only for a biological sub-subspecies of *Homo sapiens.*

**rites of passage** Supernatural ceremonies designed to help individuals pass from one stage of a life-cycle to another.

**role** The specific way of living or behaving that the members of a society expect of people holding a given **status.** Sometimes regarded as the dynamic aspect of a **status.**

**rotary power** Circular, rather than straight, power, most often associated with wheels.

**rotating forearm** That feature of **Primate** skeletal anatomy by which the radius can be made to slide over the ulna. This makes it possible for the forearm, together with the wrist and hand, to be rotated so that the palm can be held facing up, down, or to either side.

**samurai** Japanese nobles and fighting men of the past, who were allowed to wear two swords as a token of their **status.**

**seal** An engraved or inscribed stamp used for identification or signature. In Copper-Bronze days seals were frequently pressed into a soft substance that later hardened.

**secret societies Associations** of people who keep at least some of their rites or activities secret from the nonmembers of their society.

**sexual dichotomy** The sociocultural assignment of tasks to one sex or the other.

**shaman** An individual, thought to be heavily endowed with **mana.** Since he customarily uses his supernatural power to cure the sick or to counteract witchcraft, he is often equated with a **medicine man.** Originally, the word was restricted to certain Siberian tribes, but today it is universally used.

**shifting cultivators** Farmers who move from time to time.

**siblings** Children of the same parents, such as brothers or sisters. May be of one sex or both.

**Sinanthropus pekinensis** One of the **Archanthropinae,** as classified by Weidenreich. Its name means "Chinese man from Peking." It was found in a limestone quarry at Chou Kou Tien, about forty miles from Peking.

**social anthropology** A phrase widely used by British anthropologists to connote very largely what American students of man call "**cultural anthropology.**" Social anthropologists may emphasize the human beings who interact in certain ways, whereas cultural anthropologists may stress the configurations of group living that prevail in various societies.

**social conscience** Each individual's recognition of the cultural values that exist in his society or subculture. See **value interiorization.**

**sodality** An **association** or group of people who may or may not be **consanguineous** kin. See **association** and **secret society.**

**Solutrian** A late phase of Western Europe's **Paleolithic Age.**

**somatotonic** Descriptive of an individual who likes to use his body vigorously even to the extent of being aggressive. This kind of temperament is believed by Sheldon to prevail in people of **mesomorphic** build.

**somatotyping** Sheldon's method of classifying human bodies in terms of structural components rather than by virtue of racial traits.

**sororate** The cultural convention of expecting a widower to marry one of his late wife's sisters. See **levirate.**

**South-African man-apes** See **Australopithecinae.**

**spear-thrower** An instrument for hurling a spear, which has the effect of extending the user's arm by the length of the spear-thrower.

**status** See **achieved status** and **ascribed status.**

**stereoscopic** A type of vision in which the images entering from the left and right eyes overlap to produce a sense of depth. In the higher **Primates** the sense of depth may be produced even when the object that is seen is only a few inches away from the viewer.

**stimulus diffusion** The spread of an idea or stimulus from one place or culture area to another. The final products based on transmitted ideas or stimuli are not necessarily identical.

**stock** As it is used in this text, a biological subspecies of *Homo sapiens.*

**stop-ridge** A raised horizontal or transverse bar, usually placed across a celt to keep a handle from slipping downward.

**superincision** A cut formally made on the foreskin of the penis, usually as a sign of changed social status.

**supernatural sanctions** The concept that the mores of a society are backed up by supernatural powers.

**supraorbital torus** A solid bar of bone that runs across the upper margins of the eye sockets. Found in most species of apes and in some extinct **hominids.**

**surrogate** Substitute. Most often used in **cultural anthropology** with reference to substitutes for parents and other kin.

**Swanscombe man** An important type of extinct **hominid,** found in England. A number of anthropologists regard the remains as pertaining to the earliest known specimen of the **Neoanthropinae.**

**symbol** Anything to which an extrasensory value or meaning is attached by the members of a society. See **algebraic mentality.**

**tabu** A prohibition or restriction usually backed by the threat of supernatural punishment.

**talisman** An object of supernatural value, generally containing a bit of sacred writing, that is believed to help a person or to defend him from forces of evil.

**teknonymy** The custom of identifying an individual by his relationship to a third party. Usually applies to the identification of a parent through his child.

**temper** Coarse or gritty material that is worked into clay from which pottery is to be made. While the pottery is being fired the temper provides tiny outlets for the escape of gases that might otherwise cause the clay walls of a pot to crack open.

**tempering** In the manufacture of pottery, this term refers to the device of adding **temper** to clay. In the making of iron implements, tempering refers to the hardening of the material by sudden changes of temperature. See **forging**.

**territoriality** The habit of many animals of keeping intruders out of any territory that they claim for themselves. Such behavior may possibly apply to **hominids** under certain circumstances.

**tetrapods** Land animals that go about on all fours and breathe atmospheric oxygen.

**torus** See **supraorbital torus**.

**totem** An object, plant, or animal with which a social unit feels itself to be intimately connected. Sometimes, members of a **lineage** or **clan** may engage in art forms or ceremonies that express their relationship to a totem.

**tribal initiation** One or more rituals, usually designed for males, that fit individuals for completely adult roles in their society. Frequently, but not invariably, tribal initiations are puberty ceremonies in **rites of passage**.

**tropes** Portions of Christian services that are sung or enacted in church.

**true arch** An arch of two sides, each capable of supporting its own weight without overlaps, held together by a keystone. Contrast **corbeled arch**.

**unilateral** One-sided. Has reference to the tracing of relationship through one parent only, a common way of labeling kindred in primitive societies.

**unilineal** See **unilateral**.

**unilocal household** A unit of kinfolk formed when a newly wedded pair, and such offspring as may later be born to them, move into the **household group** of either principal and are terminologically merged with the kin who already reside there.

**unilocal residence** The custom of postmarital residence whereby a bridal pair moves into a home already occupied by the relatives of either party to the marriage.

**uxorilocal residence** The same as **matrilocal** residence.

**value interiorization** The presumed process by which a child takes into itself the cultural values of its society. See **enculturation**.

**varve rings** Twin layers of silt and clay that are deposited annually in lake beds by melting ice. Varve ring counts are sometimes used for establishing dates. This method has been most systematically employed by Scandinavian **archeologists**.

**virilocal residence** The same as **patrilocal** residence.

**viscerotonic** Descriptive of people interested in the stomach and the process of digestion. Usually of **endomorphic** build.

**weregild** A custom that permits a murderer to escape further punishment by the payment of money to the surviving kin of his victim.

**witch** A person of either sex who uses supernatural power for harmful or antisocial purposes.

**Würm** The last extensive outflowing movement of ice during Europe's Pleistocene.

**zoological animism** A belief in the supernatural qualities of animals. A cornerstone of primitive religion.

# INDEX OF TRIBES, SOCIETIES, AND CULTURES

Italic numbers refer to figures.

Algonkian-speaking Indians, 334 *fn.*
American, 248, 277, *12.5*, 406, 438, 420-435. *See also* New World, United States of America
Apache Indians, 371
Aranda; Arunta, 275-277, *12.4*, 285
Araucanian Indians, 199, 274, 282, 378, 398-399
Ashanti, 285
Australians (aboriginal), 236
Aztec Indians, 178, 394

Babylonians, 99
Bali; Balinese, 326, *18.2*, 412 *fn.*
Blackfoot Indians, *6.5*
Bush Negroes, 233, 370

China; Chinese, 223, 247, 250, 278, 282, 303, 360, 374, 394
Cherokee Indians, 402, 402 *fn.*, *18.9*
Crow Indian military societies, 292-293
Crow Indians, 218, 218 *fn.*, 292-293

Dahomean; Dahomey, *3.9*

Eskimo, *3.10*, 229, *10.2*, 374, 377, 401

Fiji; Fijian, *1.2*, 406 *fn.*

Hindu, 81, 99, 225, 247
Hittite, 168
Hopi Indians, 213, 218, 219, 223, 228, *10.4*, 237, *10.7*, 240, *10.8*, 257, 271, 282, 294-295, 320 *fn.*, *16.1*, 344, 374, *18.3*, 339, 389, 391, 403, 413-420, *19.2*, 429, 438

Ifugao, *13.6*
Inca Indians, 177, *7.9*, 177 *fn.*, 178
Iranian (Persian), *10.6*, *18.6*
Iroquois Indians, 259

Japanese, 223, 225, 237, 279, 300, 313-314, *15.4*, 359 *fn.*, 374, 434
Jewish; Jews, 81, 287-288, 332, 355, 377. *See also* Orthodox Jews

Korean, *1.2*, 223
Kwakiutl Indians, 290-291, *13.1*

Mapuche. *See* Araucanian
Masai, 232, 291-292, *13.2*
Masai Warriors' Societies, 291-292, *13.2*, 298
Maya Indians, 99, 175, *7.8*, 178, 394, *18.7*
Moslem, 332, 334 *fn.*, 339, *18.5 D*

Navaho Indians, 223, 228, *10.1*, *10.8*, 240, 257, 282, 311, 371, 394, *18.5 A*, 438
Nayar, 279

Old Oraibi. *See* Hopi Indians
Ona, 226, 229, *10.2*
Orthodox Jewish, 210, 218, 228, 239

Plains Cree Indians, 297, 297 *fn.*
Pomo Indians, *6.4*
Pueblo Indians, *10.1*, 233

Saramacca. *See* Bush Negroes
Shoshonean. *See* Uto-Aztecan
Sioux Indians, *3.10*, 334 *fn.*, 400

Tarahumara Indians, 239
Tikopia, 405, 406-413, *19.1*, 429
Toda, 277, 303
Trobriand Islanders, 227

United States of America, *8.8*, 203, 204, 207, 219, 226, 227, 233, 237, 248, 255, *11.4*, 257, 260, 300, 313, 326, 330-331, *15.1*, 339, 346-347, 348, 368, 372, 420 *fn.*, 434, 441. *See also* American
Uto-Aztecan, 413

Witoto Indians, *10.5*, *15.3*

Yankee City, 432-433
Yir Yoront, 20, 20 *fn.*

Zuni Indian pueblo, 282

# INDEX

Italic numbers refer to figures. Tribes, societies, and cultures are listed on p. 456.

Abbevillian, 109, 110, 112
abstraction, 97, 98, 216, 219-220, 366-367, 378, 381, 389
acculturation, 197, 197 fn., 198-200, 413. *See also* culture change
Acheulian, 109, 110-111, 112, 117
action anthropology, 435
adze, 112, 136, *6.1*
aerophones, 386, *18.1. See also* music
affinal relationships, 272-273, 289, 410, 411, 418 fn.
afterlife, 118, 130, 359, 364. *See also* other world
age-area, 252
age-groups; age-sets, 297-298
agriculture, 140, 145, 146-147, 149, 151, 154, 157, 167, 187, *8.3. See* farmers
Ainu, 76, *3.8*
Alexander the Great, 172
algebraic mentality, 99, 99 fn., 103-106, *4.7*, 113, 118, 125, 130, 149, 226, 334, 364, 367, 438
alphabet, 84, 164, 169, 182
Alpine, 76, *3.8*
Altamira, 131, *5.13, 5.14*
alternate-generation harmony, *12.4*, 284, 285, 411
American Indians. *See* Mongoloid stock
amphibian, 33, *2.4*, 55, 56, 87
amulet, 358
ancestor worship, 360, 407
Angel, J. L., 60 fn.
Angkor Wat, 394
animal domestication, 137, 137 fn., 145-146, 151, 157
animatism, animism, 336-337
Antelope society, 419
Anthropoidea, 44
ape, 39, 47-53, *2.14, 2.15, 2.16, 2.17,* 54, 56, 57, 62, *3.4 A,* 101, *4.6,* 102, 103, 104, 107, 107 fn.
ape-men. *See* Australopithecinae
Apollonian, 217, 218, 320, 417, 438
arch, 229, 230
Archaic White, 76, *3.8*
Archanthropinae, 64-66, *3.4,* 70, 71
archeology, 4, 19, 107-108, 181, 182, 184, 190, 207, 209, 254, 373, 398, 435, 437, 440-441
Archeozoic, *1.4,* 21
Aristotle, 172
Armenoid, 76

art: Aurignacian, 121-125; Magdalenian, 130-132, 138, 145
articulate speech, 368
artifact, 4, 91, 92
Aryan, 81
associations, 289-295, 304
asymmetrical evolution, 63, 63 fn., *4.1*
Aurignacian, 119, *5.4 A,* 120-125, 127, 134
Australoid, 74 fn., 76
Australopithecinae, 59-60, *3.3,* 104, 105
avoidance, 282, 408
ax. *See* fist-ax
Azoic, 21, *1.4*

baboon, 45
ball courts, 398, *18.7*
Banks Islands Sukwe, 293, *13.3,* 299
baraka, 335 fn. *See also* mana
Barnett, H. G., 197 fn.
basic personality type, 325-326
basketry, 147, *6.4,* 151, 154, 174, 415
Batak, *3.10*
Bateson, G., 257
Beals, R. L., 223 fn.
beer, 157, 226
Benedict, R. F., 217, 217 fn., 307, 320
bent-knee gait, 68, *3.4*
berdache, 242
Bering Straits, 174
betel nut, 407, 408
bifurcate-merging, 267 fn.
bilateral symmetry, 31, 32, 55
binocular vision. *See* stereoscopic vision
biocultural triangle, 194-196, *8.6,* 227, 228, 233, 261, 298, 329, 366, *19.4,* 429, 437. *See also* culture, configurations of
biocultural unconformity, 200, *8.7,* 203, 204, 205, 322
bioculture, *1.1, 1.3,* 17, 84, 87, 97, 183, *8.7,* 202, 203, 221, 223, 226, 249, 258, 261, 262, 299, 327, 348, 364, 396, *19.4,* 429, 434, 436, 437, 438, 440. *See also* culture, configurations of
biological imperatives, 25-27, 54, 55, 96, 394, 436
biophysicochemical, 7, 7 fn., 11, 15, 26, 35, 96, 97, 181, 182, 224, 231, 245, 334, 438
blade, 120, *5.4,* 126
blood-brotherhood, 297

blood-feud, 301
blood relationship. *See* consanguinity
Bloomfield, L., 368
Boas, F., 3, 83 *fn.*, 290, 368, 391
boat. *See* canoe; boat
Borobodur, 394, *18.5 D*
bow and arrow, 128, *5.12*, 130, 140, 174, 182
brachiation, 45, 47, 48, *2.14*, 53, 54, 57
Braidwood, R. J., 120 *fn.*
brain, 32, 36, 36 *fn.*, 41, 42, 44, 45, 46, 47, 52, 55, 56, 60, 63, *4.1*, 89, 92, 103, 104, 105, 106, 186
breadfruit, 407
bride-price, 274
bronze, *18.5 C. See also* Copper-Bronze Age
Broom, L., 197 *fn.*
Broom, R., 60 *fn.*
Bruner, E. M., 197 *fn.*
bucket (metallic), 169
Buddha; Buddhist, 332, *18.5 D*
Bunzel, R. L., 197 *fn.*
Bureau of Indian Affairs, 433
Bushmen, 79
butterfly-wings, 237, *10.7*

Caesar, 172
calendar, 165, 175, 178, 182, 352-354, *16.1*, 419
calendrical rites, 350 *ff.*, 400-401, 418, 419, 429
Cannibal society, 290-291, *13.1*
canoe; boat, 137, 140, 163, 182
cards, 396, 400
Carpenter, C. R., 255
carving, 391. *See also* plastic arts
cast; casting. *See* mold
caste, 250-251
Catarrhini, 45-47, *2.12 B*, 57, 172
Caucasoid (stock), 76, *3.8, 3.9*, 82, 83, 167, 210, 223, 398, 425
cell, 27, *2.1, 2.2*, 28, 29, 31, 44, 55, 73, 104, 106
celt, 142, *6.3*, 161, *7.4*
Cenozoic, *1.4*, 21, 38, 56
ceramics. *See* pottery
cerebellum, 44
cerebral cortex, 35, 36, 36 *fn.*, 37, 41, 56, 103
cerebrotonic, 203 *fn.*, 320
cerebrum, 35, 44
ceremonial calendar, 352-356, *16.1*, 363, 391. *See also* calendrical rites
ceremonial coyness, 273
ceremonial parents, 297, 418
Chamberlin, A. F., 3
Chapple, E. D., 223 *fn.*, 434, 434 *fn.*, 435
chariot, 169, 170, *7.7*
charm, 358; vocalized, 377
checkers, 396, 399
Chellian. *See* Abbevillian
chess, 396, 399
Childe, V. G., 144, 144 *fn.*, 150
chimpanzee, 8, *2.7*, 47, 49-50, *2.16*, 93, *4.4, 4.5*, 95, 101, *4.6*, 107, 107 *fn.*
Chimp-O-Mat, 95, *4.5*
chin, 49, 52, *2.18*
chisel, 136
chocolate, 84, 224
chopper, *5.2 C*, 112, 113
chopsticks, 10, *1.2*, 225, 257

chordophones, 386. *See also* music
Chou Kou Tien, 66
Choukoutienian industry, 112, 112 *fn.*
Christmas, 352, 355
chromosome, 28, 29
Cicero, 172
circumcision, 291
cire-perdue method, 159
clan; clanmates, 266, 267, 269, 271, 274, 275, 303, 413, 415, 416, 416 *fn.*, 417, 418 *fn.*, 428
class, 250, 432-433
classificatory nomenclature, 265, 275, 303. *See also* kinship
clavicle, 40, *2.9, 4.3*, 91, 130
cleaver, 111, 113
clitoridectomy, 291
clothing, 3, 233-239, *10.5, 10.6, 10.7, 13.1*, 294, *13.4*, 295, *13.5*, 338, *15.3*, 378, *18.3*, 391, 407
clowns, 363
cocaine, 179
cocoa, 84, 224
Codrington, R. H., 334 *fn.*
coiling, 148
coinage; coins, 164, 169, 182, *8.3*, 400
cold-bloodedness, 32, 36
collarbone. *See* clavicle
Collier, J., 433
concubinage; concubine, 278, 278 *fn.*
consanguinity, 272, 273, 274, 282, 289, 303, 359, 410
conscience, 315
contagion (religious), 336, 348
controlled causation, law of, 345-348, *15.6*, 400, 426, 437
Coon, C. S., 223 *fn.*
copper, 142, 153-154, 158, 160, 162, 163, 167, 177, 177 *fn. See also* Copper-Bronze Age
Copper-Bronze Age, *6.5*, 154-167, 168, 169, 175, 177, 237
copulation, 8, 35, 56
corbeled (false) arch, 229-230
core-built ax, 136
core tools, 110, 111, 112, 114, 115, 120, 142
corn. *See* maize
cortex. *See* cerebral cortex
costumes. *See* clothing
co-tradition, 254
cotton gin, 422-423
council of elders, 359 *fn.*
counting coup, 288
*coup de poing. See* fist-ax
couvade, 299
covert patterns (of culture), 221, 227
cranial capacity, 47, 47 *fn.*, 48, 49, 52, 60, 63, 65, 66, 70, 92, 104, 105, *4.7. See also* brain
cremation, 169
critical point, 104, 105, *4.7*
critical rites, 350 *ff.*, 400-401, 419, 429
critical threshold, 104, 105, *4.7*
Cro-Magnon, 70, 71, *3.5*, 119
cross-cousins; cross-cousin marriage, 273-274, 275, *12.4*, 284, 285, 416
Crossopterygian, 33, *2.4*
Crow system of nomenclature, 267, *12.3*, 269, 284, 303. *See also* kinship
cryptocrystalline, 113, 142

Culin, S., 399, 399 *fn.*
cultural blindness, 242-243, 408
cultural dynamics. *See* dynamics
cultural relativism, 441
cultural stereotype, 202
culture, configurations of, 194-196, 217, 221, 223, 254, 306, 330, 364, *19.4,* 434, 437, 438, 441. *See also* patterns of culture
culture area, 251-255, *11.3,* 387
culture change, 196-200, 220, 367, 387, 406, 437, 439. *See also* acculturation
cuneiform, 164-165

dance; dancing, 341, 347, 387-391, *18.2, 18.3,* 408, *19.1,* 418, 419
Darius, 170
Darwin, C. R., 2, 3, 64
death, origin of, 361-362, 376
descriptive nomenclature, 265, 303. *See also* kinship
Devonian Age, *1.4,* 33, 55
dialect, 371
diastema, *3.3*
dice, 396, *18.6,* 400
Dickinson, E., 97, 334
diffusion, 135, 145, 179, 197, 372, 373, 387, 420
Dinaric, 76
Dinka, *3.9*
Dionysian, 217, 218, 320, 438
discovery, 149
diviner; divination, 341 *fn., 15.5. See also* mantic "science"
dog, 137, 140, *6.5,* 174, *8.3*
Dordogne, *5.8,* 124, *5.9*
dowry, 274
drama, 341, 378-379
Dubois, C., vi
Dubois, E., 64, 66
duck, 179
Duk-Duk society, *13.5*
Dunn, L. C., 83 *fn.*
dynamics, cultural or biocultural, 185, 198, 200, 228, 306, 330, 347, 364, 399, 439-440
dysphoria, 200

Eastern Mediterranean Zone, 141, 151, 153, 157, 167, 168, 172
ectomorph; ectomorphic, 203 *fn.,* 320, *14.3*
Eggan, F., *12.2,* 275
emancipation of the forelimbs, 90, 92
enculturation, 12, 310-315, *14.1,* 316, 318, 319, 323, 324
endogamy, 263
endomorph; endomorphic, 203 *fn.*
engraving, 391. *See also* graphic arts
Eocene, *1.4,* 41
eolith, 107, *5.1*
Ertebølle, 137-138, *6.2. See also* Mesolithic
Esperanto, 373
esthetics, 231, 342, 383, 384, 387, 388, 391, 392, 394, 421
ethics. *See* moral code
ethnomusicology, 385, 385 *fn.*
etiquette, 225, 226, *11.1*
Eutheria(n). *See* placenta(l)

evolution: cultural, 125, 130, 137, 140, 154, 172, 173, 175, 184, 215, 254, 288, 436; organic, vi, 2, 3, 20, *1.4,* 21, 30, *2.3,* 31, *2.4,* 41, 45, 54, 56, 57, 67 *fn.,* 72, 82, 87, 91, 172, 175, 436
exogamy, 263, 273, 274, 275, 289, 304, 413, 418 *fn.*
extended family, 272
extinct hominids, 63-71, 104, 172
extrabiological, 3, 9, 11, 12, 81, 87, *4.2,* 92, 93, 125, 130, 185, 193, 226, 423, 436
extrasomatic. *See* extrabiological

family, 41, 60, 271, 272, 303, 411, 416; of orientation, 272, 313, *14.2;* of procreation, 272, 313, *14.2*
farmers; farming, 345-346, 353-354, 408, 413-414, 422. *See also* agriculture
Fejos, P., *10.5, 15.3*
femur, 62, 65, 66, *3.4 A*
fetish, 358
fibula: anatomical, 62; archeological, 160, *7.3,* 169
fine arts. *See* esthetics
first-fruit rites, 355-356, 363, 407
Firth, R., 406 *fn.,* 413
Fischer, E., 83 *fn.*
fish; fishing, 31, 32, 33, *2.4,* 35, 55, 56, 224, 252, 255, 407, 408, 411
fist-ax, 110, *5.2 A,* 111, 113, 114, 117, 118, 136
flake tools, 111, 114, 117, 120, 142
Flute societies, 419
folk societies, 433
folklore, 375-376, 378
Fontéchevade man, 69 *fn.*
foramen magnum, *2.18,* 62
force, vi, 14-18, 23, 24, 185, 193-194, 200, *8.7,* 228, 245, *11.1,* 261, 298, 306, 333, 335, 336, 359, 361, 388, 399, 439, 440
foresight. *See* prediction
Forest Negro, 79, *3.9*
forging, 168-169
Foster, G. M., 224, 224 *fn.*
fossil man. *See* hominid, extinct
Foxes, 292-293
Freud, S.; Freudian, 32, 307, 311
friendship, 296-298, 304

gambling, 396, 399
games, 342, 394-403, 408
Garn, S., 82 *fn.*
geisha, 279
gene; genetic, 28, 29, 73, 83, 261, 283, 303, 317
genetics, 76, 82 *fn.* 83, 309, 318, 319, 439
genotypical, 73
gens, 266. *See also* clan
Gerard, R. W., 91
gerontocracy, 359 *fn.*
Gesell, A., 312, 317
ghost gamble, 400. *See also* gambling
giants, 64, 64 *fn.,* 70
gibbon, 47-48, *2.14,* 53, 57
Gillin, J., 224 *fn.*
glottochronology, 372, 372 *fns.,* 373
godparents, 296

gods, 339-340, *15.4,* 345, 381, 391, *18.5 A,* 399, 403, 407, 410
Goodenough, W., vi
Gorer, G., 420 *fn.*
gorilla, 8, 47, *2.17,* 53, 62, 104
graphic arts, 391-394
Griffin, J. B., vi
grinding technique. *See* polishing technique
Gua, 101, *4.6,* 102
Gunther, E., 356 *fn.*

Haddon, A. C., 391, 391 *fn.*
haft; hafting, 117, 118, 128, 136, *6.1,* 140, 142, 161-162, *7.4*
Hallowell, A. I., 307
Hambly, W. D., 388 *fn.*
hand-adze. *See* adze
hand-ax. *See* fist-ax
handle. *See* haft
Hanukka, 355
Hawthorne plant, 432, 434
hearing, 33, 37, 56
hemoglobin, 32, 37
Henry, J., 212 *fn.*
Herodotus, 170
Herskovits, M. J., 12 *fn.,* 197 *fn.,* 233, 233 *fn.,* 251, 309, 392 *fn.*
Herzog, E., 218 *fn.*
heterodont, 36, 56
heterosis, 82
Hewes, G. C., *10.3,* 257
hieroglyphics, 176, *7.8*
Hippocrates, 170
Hoebel, E. A., 298 *fn.*
Hoijer, H., 223 *fn.,* 372
Holocene period, *1.4,* 119
Homegoing dance, *18.3*
hominids, 8, 19, 21, 45, 53, 54, 63, 64, 66, *3.4 A,* 68, 70, 76, 93, 107, 109, 114, 172, 185, *8.2,* 193, 242, 271; extinct, 63-71, 104, 172
homodont, 36, 56
*Homo neandertalensis. See* Neandertal man
*Homo sapiens,* 3, 5, 7, 9, 10, 11, 12, 13, 19, 20, 21, 27, 32, 38, 41, 49, 61, 63, 72, 73, 74, 76, 79, 86, 87, 89, 90, 92, 103, 103 *fn.,* 115, 125, 130, 135, 138, 142, 167, 172, 179, 181, *8.2,* 187, 209, 222, 245, 247, 248, 255, 271, 309, 317, 329, 405, 428, 433, 436, 437, 440
homosexual, 204, 323, 324
Hooton, E. A., *2.6,* 53 *fn.,* 63 *fn.*
hormone, 25, 279
horse, 157, *7.7,* 178, 179
Hotevilla, 403. *See also* Hopi Indians
Hottentot, 79, *3.9,* 83
houses, 3, 146, 175, 190, 228-233, 252, *11.3,* 394, *18.5 D,* 407, 408, 412-413, 415, 421, 423, *19.3*
Howell, F. C., 67 *fn.*
Howells, W. W., *2.18*
howler monkey, *2.12 A,* 255
Hrdlička, A., 173
human muscular energy, conservation of, 114, 191-193, 250, 421, 423, 439
hybrid vigor, 82

idiophones, 386. *See also* music

idol, 358, 388
igloo, 230
imitation magic. *See* mimetic magic
inbreeding, 73, 76, 83
incest, 2, 262, 273, 274, 284, 285, 289, 304
independent invention, 99, 179, 371
Indo-European, 368, 374
Indonesian-Malay, *3.10,* 81
infanticide, 265, 300, 411, 429
initiation by trespass, 418-419
institution (cultural) 193-194, 261, 326, 439-440
interaction chronograph, 434 *fn.*
interiorizing (of values), 315-318, 319, 324, 438
internal consistency, 213
invention, 149, 387
invertebrate, 31, 33, 55
Iron Age, 154, 168-172, 178
Islamic, 81, *10.6*
Ituri forest pygmy, *3.9*

javelin. *See* spear
javelin-thrower. *See* spear-thrower
jellyfish, 55
joint family, 272
joking relationship, 275

Kachina, 389-391, *18.3,* 418-419. *See also* Hopi Indians
kava, 407
Kellogg ape-child experiment, 101, *4.6*
Kinsey, A. C., 279
kinship, 262, 265, *12.1,* 274, 275, 283-285, 289, 298, 410, 416, 422
kinship sets, 285
kitchen midden, 137, 138, 149
kiva, 233, *10.4,* 418
Kluckhohn, C., 221, 221 *fn.,* 307, 373, 373 *fn.,* 420 *fn.,* 433 *fn.*
Kluckhohn, F., 212 *fn.*
knife: stone, 111, *5.2 B,* 113; iron, 169, 170, *7.7,* 190, 257. *See also* side-scraper
Köhler, W., 99 *fn.*
Koran, 339
kris, 237, *18.2*
Kroeber, A. L., 174, 220, 220 *fn.,* 252, 253, 394, 397
Krogman, W. M., 72, 73 *fn.,* 74 *fn.*

LaBarre, W., 257 *fn.*
La Chapelle-aux-Saints, *3.4,* 118
lacrosse, 402, *18.9*
Lakon society, 419
language. *See* linguistics
Lascaux, 124, 124 *fn.,* *5.9,* 130
Lasker, G. W., 60 *fn.*
Latin, 81
Laughlin, W. S., 174 *fn.*
laurel-leafed blades. *See* Solutrian
law (primitive), 298-302
law of controlled causation. *See* controlled causation, law of
laying on of hands, 336, *15.2*
learning theory, 308
Lee, D., 380 *fn.*
legend, 375
Leighton, A. H., 434 *fn.*

lemur, Lemuroidea, 39, 41-42, *2.10*, 44, 56, 57, 172
Les Eyzies, 124, 130
Levallois technique, 111, 112, *5.3*, 117
levirate, 273, 411
lexicostatistics. *See* glottochronology
lineage, 266, *12.2*, 267, *12.6*
linguistics, 3, 5, 210-211, 366-375, 379
Linnaeus, 56
Linton, R., 73 *fn.*, 249, 280, 307
llama, 175
local invention. *See* independent invention
loom, 147
lost-wax method, 159
Lower Paleolithic, 109-115, 136, 185
Lowie, R. H., 218 *fn.*, 275
luck; lucky, 399, 400, 402
Lumholtz, C., 239, 239 *fn.*
Lumpwoods, 292-293
Lynd, H. M., 425, 426, 426 *fn.*, 431, 431 *fn.*
Lynd, R. S., 425, 426, 426 *fn.*, 431, 431 *fn.*

Macacque monkey, *2.12*, 45
Magdalenian, 119, *5.4 B*, 120, 127-133, 134
magic, 344 *fn.*, 350-352; mimetic, 131, 354, 400
Maglemose, 136-137. *See also* Mesolithic
Maier, N. R. F., 322, 322 *fn.*, 323
maize, 175, 179, 224, 415
Malinowski, B., 227 *fn.*, 388 *fn.*
mammal, 8, 36, 37, 38, 39, 56, 86, 255, 394
mana, 334-336, 338, 341, 343, 344, 354, 360, 363, 388, 402
man-apes. *See* Australopithecinae
Mandelbaum, D. G., 297 *fn.*
mandible, 32, 47, 49, 52
manioc, 246, *11.2*
Manitou, 334 *fn. See also* mana
mantic "science," 341. *See also* prediction
Marau society, *10.4*, 294-295, *13.4*, 297, 419
Marett, R. R., 337
marital frigidity, 324
masks, 387, 394, 419. *See also* Kachina
mass production, 158
material culture. *See* technology
mathematics, 84, 164, 167, 175, 177, *8.3*
matrilineal. *See* clans; lineages
matrilocal residence, 280, *12.6*, 282, 284, 303, 415
Mayo, E., 432
Mead, M., 257, 307, 412 *fn.*, 420 *fn.*
measurements (bodily), 74, *3.6*, 76
medicine man. *See* shaman
Mediterranean (race), 76, *3.8*, 167
Melanesia, 406, 406 *fn.*
membraphones, 386. *See also* music
menstrual; menstruation, 44, 47, 232, 240, 279, 358, 358 *fn.*, 411, 411 *fn.*, 417
Mesolithic, 134-138, 140, 141, 144, 150, 154, 174, 175, 436
mesomorph; mesomorphic, 203 *fn.*, 320, *14.3*
Mesozoic, *1.4*, 21
metal; metallurgy, 142, 153-172, 175, 177 *fn.*, 178, 187, *8.3*, 190, 198, 394, 436
Metazoa, 31, 55
microlith, 127, 128, 136
Middle Paleolithic. *See* Mousterian

Middle Stone Age. *See* Mesolithic
mimetic magic, 131, 354, 400
mine; mining, 142-143
Miner, H. M., 339, 339 *fn.*
Miocene, *1.4*, 47, 53
modal personality type, 325-326
Mohammedan, 81, *10.6*
moiety, 270, 275, 303
mold; molding, 152, 158, *7.2*
Mongoloid (epicanthic) fold, *3.7*, 79, *3.10*
Mongoloid spot, 81
Mongoloid stock, 79, *3.10*, 82, 84, 167, 405, 425
monkey, 39, 44-47, 53, 56
monogamy, 288, 304
Mooney, J., 402 *fn.*
moral code, 3, 11, 150, 217 *fn.*, 262, 333, 338
morpheme, 369
motor habits, 198, *10.3*, 255-258, *11.4*, *11.5*, 318, 367, 438
mourning, 360, *16.3*, 361
Mousterian, 68, 115-118, *5.3*, 119, 121, 125, 128
Mousterian points, *5.3*, 117
Movius, H. L. Jr., 112, 112 *fn.*
multilocal household, 280
Murdock, G. P., 275 *fn.*, 288
Murphy, R., vi
music, 385-387, *18.1*, 388, 418
Muslim, 81, *10.6*
mutton, 224
myth, 361, 364, 375

names; nicknames, 380-381
nasal bones, 52, *2.18*, *3.3*
natal household kin, 284, 304, 410, 411, 412
national character, 326-327, 420 *fn.*
Neandertal man, 66, 67, 67 *fn.*, 68, 69 *fn.*, *3.4*, 70, 71, *3.5*, 115-118, *5.3*, 119
Negroid (stock), 76, *3.9*, 79, 82, 83, 167, 405, 423, 425
Neoanthropinae, 64, 68-71, 119, 127
Neolithic, 138, 139-152, 154, 155, 157, 158, 162, 167, 175, 190, 209
neolocal residence, 280, 303
neonate, 7, 11, 283, 310, *14.1*, 311, 316, 317, 319, 322
neopallium. *See* cerebral cortex
Nettl, B., 387 *fn.*
new-fire rites, 354-355, 363
New Stone Age. *See* Neolithic
New Testament, 343 *fn.*
New World, 41, 44, 45, *2.13*, 57, 167, 172-180, 398. *See also* American; United States of America
New World monkeys. *See* Platyrrhini
New Year, 355
night soil, 242
Nilotic, 79, *3.9*
Niman kachina dance, *18.3*
nonbiological. *See* extrabiological
Nordic, 76, *3.8*
nuchal musculature, *2.18*, 62, 66
nucleus, 27

Oaqöl society, 419
observations (bodily), 74, *3.7*, 76
occipital, 62, 65

Oceanic Negro, 79, *3.9*
Oedipus complex, 311
Old Stone Age. *See* Paleolithic
Old Testament, 335, 335 *fn.*
Oligocene, *1.4*, 44, 53
Omaha, 267, *12.1*, 269, 284, 303. *See also* kinship
Opler, M. E., 218, 218 *fn.*
opposable thumb, 39, *2.7*, *4.2*
orangutan, 8, 47, 48-49, *2.15*
orator; oratory, 380
ordeal, 301, *13.6*, 400, 402
orenda, 334 *fn. See also* mana
orthograde, *2.16*, *4.1*, 89
other world, *16.2*, 360, 362, *16.4*. *See also* afterlife
overt patterns of culture, 221, 425

Padrino groups, 296
painting, 387, 391, 394, *18.5*
Paleoanthropinae, 64, 66-68, 70, 119
Paleolithic, 108, 109-133, 135, 138, 140, 141, 142, 150, 154, 175, 190, 191, 383, 436
Paleozoic, *1.4*, 21, 33, 55
palstave, *7.4*, 161
pandanus, 407
Panpipe, 386, *18.1*
Papuan, *3.9*
parallel cousin, 274
participant-observer, 212, 212 *fn.*, 413
patrilineal. *See* clans; lineages
patrilocal residence, 280, 282, 284, 303, 410
pattern(s) of culture, 217, 217 *fn.*, 218, 271, 306, 309, 317, 318, 319, 322, 326, 327, 329, 333, 353, 366, 375, 387, 406, 417, 430, 434, 435, 437, 440, 441. *See also* culture, configurations of
Paul, B. D., 212 *fn.*
peasant societies, 433
percussion technique, 110, 113, 117, 141, 142
personality, 306, 307, 308, 309, 311, 315, 319, 322, 323, 323 *fn.*, 325, 326, 327, 434-435, 438
phase, 254
phenotypical, 73, 82
phoneme, 369, 371, 371 *fn.*
phratry, 269-270, 303
physical anthropologists, 3, 59, *3.3*, 81, 207, 435, 440
pick, 136
Pike, K. L., vi, 366 *fn.*
*piki*, 415
Piltdown man (*Eoanthropus dawsoni*), 68 *fn.*
*Pithecanthropus erectus*, 65-66, *3.4 A*, 70
placenta(l), 8, 38, *2.6*, 39, 56, 86
plant domestication. *See* agriculture
plastic arts, 391-394
plasticity (racial), 82
Platyrrhine; Platyrrhini, 44, *2.12*, *2.13*, 45, 57, 172
Pleistocene, *1.4*, 60, 64, 66, 67, 68, 69, 70, 71, 93, 108, 109, 127, 132, 134, 135, 173, 173 *fn.*
Pliocene, *1.4*, 60
poetry, 376, 377, 378, 388
polishing technique, 141-142, 152, 174
polyandry, 277
polygamy, 277, 288, 304

polygyny, 277, 288, 412
Polynesia, 406, 406 *fn.*
potato, 175, 179
potter; pottery, 1, 38, *6.2*, 140, 143-145, 151, 152, 154, 155, *7.1*, 175, 187, 196, 367, 384, *18.5 B*, 415
Powamu society, 419
Powdermaker, H., vi
prayer, 340, 341, 351, 376, 387, 399, 418
prediction, 1, 38, 93-94, 96, 111, 113, 121, *5.12*, 130, 143, 145, 149, 220, 397, 437, 440
prehensile grip, 39, *2.7*, *2.9*, *2.14*, *2.15*
prehensile tail, 45, *2.13*
pressure-flaking, 113, 126, *5.10*, 141, 142
Primate, 8, 9, 39, *2.7*, 39-47, 52, 53, 54, 56, 57, 60, 62, 64, 86, 87, 89, 90, 91, *4.3*, 101, 102, 103, 103 *fn.*, 105, *4.7*, 107 *fn.*, 114, *5.12*, 130, 255
procession, 341, 387-388, 399
prognathism, *2.18*, *3.3*, *3.4 B*, 79
projective tests, 307-308, 327
prostitution, 87, 87 *fn.*, 204, 279
protein, 24, 25, 26
Proterozoic, *1.4*, 21
protoplasm, 25, 26, 27, 54, 222
Protozoa(n), 27, 30, 31, 55
Pygmy Negroes, 79, *3.9*, *5.12*

quinine, 84
quipu, *7.9*

race, 73, 74, 75, 76, 81-83, 182, 385, 436, 440
race mixture, 76, 82, 83, 84, 436, 440
race problems, 17, 18
racing, 398, 400
racist, 83
radius (anatomical) 40, *2.8*
razor, 169, *7.6 B*
Redfield, R., 432
reflex actions, 55
refuse mound. *See* kitchen midden
religion; religious, 3, 20, 84, 138, 149, 150, 155, 196, 227, 228, 231, 232, 241, *11.1*, 350-365, 377, 378, 384, 387, 388, 389, 391, 394, 396, 399, 400, 407, 408, 410, 411, 417-420, 426, 427, 430. *See also* algebraic mentality; supernatural; symbol
religious thrill, 333
reptile, 36, *2.5*, 56, 255
Rhesus monkey, *2.12*, 45
Rhodes, W., 385 *fn.*
rice, 224, 225
Richardson, J., 220, 220 *fn.*
rites of passage, 356-361, *16.2*, 363-364, 387
Rivers, W. H. R., 293 *fn.*
Robinson, J. T., 60 *fn.*
role, 249, 250, 283, 429
Rorschach, 308 *fn.*
rotary power. *See* wheel
rotating forearm, 40, *2.8*, *2.9*, *4.2*, 130
Rouse, I., 254 *fn.*
rubber, 84, 179
rural, 421-422

sago palm, 407
samurai, 237

sand-painting, 394, *18.5 A*
Sapir, E., 368
saw (metallic), *7.2*, 169, 190
Schultz, A. H., *2.12*
science, 1, 2, 345-348, *15.6*, 426-427, 435, 437, 439, 440
scissors, 169, *7.6 A*
scribe, 166
sculpture; sculpturing, 391, 394
scythe (metallic), *7.6 F*
seal, 164, *7.5*, 166
secret society, 232, 290, 417, 418, 497. *See also* associations
Semitic, 81, 84
sexual dichotomy, *7.1*, 240-242, *10.8*, *11.4*, 408, 415
shaman, *15.3*, 343-345, 347, 348, *18.5 A*, 419
Shapiro, H. L., 83 *fn.*
Sharp, L., 20
shears, 169, *7.6 A*
Sheldon, W. H., 203 *fn.*, 320, 320 *fn.*, *14.3*
sherd. *See* pottery
shifting cultivators, 295
shovel-shaped incisors, 79
sib, 266. *See also* clan
siblings, 262, 267, 313, 317
sickle (metallic), *7.6 E*
side-scraper, 111, *5.2 B*, 113
Siegel, B. J., 197 *fn.*
simian, 53, 54, 59, 60, 63, 70
Simiidae, 57
*Sinanthropus pekinensis*, 66, *3.4 B*, 70, 93
singing. *See* song
situla, 169
Snake society, 419
social conscience, 315
social singing, 378, 378 *fn.*
sociocultural mobility, 250
Socrates, 172
sodality, 297. *See also* secret society
solstice, 352, 353, 354, 355, 363, 419
Solutrian, 119, 125-127, 134
somatotonic, 203 *fn.*, 320, *14.3*
song, 341, 376-377, 378, 408, 418
song-tieing, 377
Sophocles, 170
sororate, 273
soul; spirit, 336, 347, *16.2*, 359, 360, 364, 401, 407, 412, 417, 419
South-African man-apes. *See* Australopithecinae
Soyal ceremony, 339, 419
spear, *5.3*, 117, 118, *5.5*, 121, 182
spear-thrower, 121, *5.6*, 127, *5.11*, 130, 174
speech, 98-99, 101, 102, 103, 199, 379, 388, 425, 439. *See also* linguistics
speech community, 371
Spicer, E. H., 20 *fn.*, 296 *fn.*
Spider monkey, 45, *2.13*
Spier, L., vi, 221 *fn.*
spirit. *See* soul
Spiro, M. E., 312 *fn.*
Split at Oraibi, 403
sports, 397-399
Spuhler, J. N., vi, 225 *fn.*
squash, 175, 415

statistics, 75, *7.9*
status, 249, 250, 376, 410, 413, 423, 429, 439
steatopygy, *3.9*
steel, 154
stereoscopic vision, 42, 45, 46, 57, 91, 92
Steward, J. H., vi
Stewart, T. D., 64 *fn.*
stimulus diffusion, 251-254. *See also* diffusion
stock, 73, 74, 74 *fn.*, 75, 76, 81, 82, 182, 436, 440
stop-ridge, 161, *7.4*
string figures, 400-401, *18.8*
subculture, 249, 327, 392, 420
Sukwe. *See* Banks Islands Sukwe
Sun Watchers, *16.1*, 419
superincision, 411
supernatural, *8.6*, 150, 196, 227, 232, 239, 273, 301-302, 304, 329-365, 376, 379, 381, 387, 388, 389, 399-403, *18.9*, 411, 412, 426, *19.4*, 429
superstition, 342, 399
supraorbital torus, 49, 52, 63, *3.3*, 65, *3.4 B*
surrogate, 263, 269, 309
Swadesh, M., 372, 372 *fn.*
swastika, 392, *18.4*
Swiss lake-dwellings, *6.3*
symbols, 97-103, 104, 105, *4.7*, 113, *5.7*, 166, 262, 283, 394, *18.5*, 399, 436, 438

tabu, 227, 282, 284, 285, 336, 338, 361, 407
talisman, 358
taro, 407
tarsier; Tarsioidea, 39, 42-44, *2.11*, 45, 56, 57, 172
Tax, S., 275, 435
technology, 20, 114, 143, 155, 167, 192, 199, 239-242, *10.8*, *11.2*, 254, 255, 421, 422, 423, *19.3*, 430
teknonymy, 270
temper; tempering: pottery, 138, 144, 145; iron, 168-169
territoriality, 255
tetrapod, 33, 56
textile. *See* weaving
Thematic Apperception Test (TAT), 308 *fn.*
thighbone. *See* femur
Thomas, W. L. Jr., 259 *fn.*
Thompson, S., 375 *fn.*
tibia, 62
time (conservation of), 114, 191-193, 421, 439
tin, 154, 162, 163, 177, 177 *fn. See also* Copper-Bronze Age
tobacco, 84, 175, 179, 418
tools, 3, 60, 66, 68, 92, 93, *4.4*, 96, 97, 113, 114, 130, 140, 142, 196
tortoise core, 111
torus. *See* supraorbital torus
totem, 267
totem pole, 394
trade; trading, 142, 151, 163
trait complex, 252
tranchet, 136
travois, *6.5*
trend, 182, 183, 193, 254, 347, 348, 441
tribal initiation, 358, 364, 419, 429
trope, 379

Tungus, *3.10*, 374
Turkey, 175, 179, 224
tweezers, 169
twined basketry, 147
Tylor, E. B., 333, 336, 396-397

ulna, 40, *2.8*
Underhill, R., 377 *fn.*
unilateral, 266, 410-411, 416, 428
unilateral cross-cousin marriage, 284
unilineal. *See* unilateral
unilocal household group, 280, *12.6*, 282
Upper Paleolithic, 119-133, 135, 392
upright posture, 53, 57, 60, 61, *3.1*, 62. *See also* orthograde
urban; urbanization, 421-423, 428
uxorilocal residence. *See* matrilocal residence

values; meanings (cultural or symbolic), 12, 200, 201, 204, 205, 207, 215, 223, 224, 225, 226, 228, 242, 245, 247, 248, 249, 299, 306, 309, 313, 324, *14.4*, 329, 334, 366, 367, 375, 378, 385, 421, 423, 424-425, 426, 436, 437, 438, 439
Van Gennep, A., 356, *16.2*
varve, 135 *fn.*
Veddoid, 76
Venus, 123, *5.8*
vertebrate, 31, 32, 33, 55, 56
virilocal residence. *See* patrilocal residence
viscerotonic, 203 *fn.*
vision, 241. *See also* stereoscopic vision
Vogt, E. Z., 197 *fn.*
Von Koenigswald, G. H. R., 65 *fn.*

wakan; wakonda, 334 *fn. See also* mana
war; warfare, 288, 304, 396
warm-blooded, 9, 36, 37, 56
Warner, W. L., 313 *fn.*, 432, 433 *fn.*, 435
warp, 147, *6.4*
War Relocation Authority, 434
Washburn, S. L., *4.1*, 89
Waterman, T. T., 397 *fn.*
Watson, J. B., 197 *fn.*
weaving, 147, 149, 151, 154, 187, *8.3*, *10.4*, 415
weft, 147
Weidenreich, F., 64, 64 *fn.*
Weiner, J. S., 68 *fn.*
Weltfish, G., 239 *fn.*, 384, 384 *fn.*
weregild, 301
Western hemisphere. *See* New World
wheel, *6.5*, 149, 154-155, *7.1*, 157, 175, 178
White, L. A., 99 *fn.*
Whorf, B. L., 373, 373 *fn.*
wife capture, 274, 411, 411 *fn.*
willow-leafed blades. *See* Solutrian
wine, 157, 170
Wissler, C., 251 *fn.*, 431
witch; witchcraft, 343-345, 354, 417, 419
woof. *See* weft
Wordsworth, W., 333
wrestling, 397-398, 408
writing, 164-165, *7.5*, 166, 169, 175, *7.8*, 177, *8.3*, 211, 392
Würm, 109, 115, 119, 126

yearly round, 214

zero, 99
Zborowski, M., 218 *fn.*

THE EASTERN MEDITERRANEAN ZO

PLACES MARKED WITH STARS INDICAT